This book belongs to

_____

BLAME IT ON REVERE!
The Portsmouth Alarm

Copyright © 2021 by Angela Welch

ISBN: 978-1-7368216-0-2
Library of Congress PCN: 2021904710

To contact to order a copy of this book,
please visit www.amitypublications.com

Layout and designed by
AMITY Publications

Printed in the United States of America

BLAME IT ON REVERE!

The Portsmouth Alarm

December 1774

Written by Angela Welch

Illustrated by Sarah Boudreau

Everyone knows of Revere's famous ride

One April night in seventy-five.

But Revere's first ride was four months before

On a cold December morning in seventy-four.

What was so urgent that Revere came forth

To saddle his horse and then journey north?

A journey requiring him to ride with haste

Knowing that there was no time to waste!

This information could not keep him inside

But the weather made for a difficult ride.

For the king and his council had passed an order

That sent Revere to the New Hampshire border.

King George made it clear there would be no more

Importation of gunpowder and military stores.

The unrest in the colonies just made no sense.

There would be nothing to use for self-defense.

General Gage was ordered to collect the lot.

All the muskets, cannon, powder and shot.

And the general was so very sure

That a large supply was in New Hampshire.

The stores were at Fort William and Mary
With six British soldiers and some artillery.
The fort in Portsmouth was a symbol of might
But more men were needed in case of a fight!

The general sent two ships to the north
To provide more men and strengthen the fort.
The Sons of Liberty were also informed.
It was time that Portsmouth was also warned.

The storm came with a howl and the winds did moan.

Revere knew he would be chilled to the bone.

The New England weather per its usual way

Made roads dangerous for travel that day.

His journey started across the Boston Neck.

Frozen roads and ruts were part of the trek.

First, he must pass the British guards.

Since they knew him, it was not so hard!

The race was on! He would beat the ships yet.

For the Boston Post road was his best bet.

Through the North Shore, across the Merrimack,

Onward he rode and he never looked back.

Through Seabrook and Hampton, he galloped fast.

Sixty-five miles almost finished at last!

He had no time to stop, no time to lose.

Portsmouth's citizens needed the news!

Revere said the British were on the way,

Two regiments of regulars without delay.

They'll follow the order and seize everything

For that was the plan of George the King.

Portsmouth's Patriots got the important news.

The Tories knew it was important, too.

Governor Wentworth received a full report

And he needed help to save that old fort.

Revere's visit to Portsmouth was not a good sign.

Wentworth didn't think there was a whole lot of time.

An express rider rode south and did his best

To give General Gage his urgent request.

The British agreed more troops needed to go

On board the Scarborough and the Canceaux.

They carried Marines and could leave right away

But a storm gave the ships a one week delay.

Meanwhile, in Portsmouth, four hundred men did come

To the tune of the fife and the beat of the drum.

In the afternoon, the men did go

By water and land, through falling white snow.

Led by John Langdon, the men did insist

That the six British soldiers shouldn't resist!

The British were outnumbered four hundred to six.

The captain told them to enter at their risk!

The Patriots did attack, one and all,

Right over the fort's old crumbling walls.

The British fired three cannons to no avail.

The triumphant Patriots did prevail.

Captain Cochran surrendered, his sword given back

But the Patriots took down the Union Jack!

Three cheers were given and they were not caught.

It was time to take out the powder and shot.

About one hundred barrels they did deliver

To Durham by the Oyster River.

Under the meeting house pulpit, much they did hide.

The rest sent to other towns with pride.

The next day, Major Sullivan returned to the fort.

He took more weapons with his cohorts.

Revere returned to Boston, his mission done.

The British were shocked, each and every one.

The two ships arrived in New Hampshire's seaport.

There were one hundred men to dismantle the fort.

The British were angered at the weather delay,

And the Patriots had long since gone away.

The Revolution had begun, but nobody knew

That the Patriots' anger continued to brew.

Governor Wentworth cried to all far and near

That he blamed it all on Paul Revere!

<u>What happened next?</u>

 Portsmouth hid 4 barrels of powder.
Durham received 25 barrels, some hidden under a church pulpit.
Exeter received 29 barrels to store in their Powder House.
Kingston took 12 barrels.
Epping and Nottingham each accepted 8 barrels.
Fremont, then known as Poplin, and Brentwood were given 4 barrels.
Londonderry took 1 barrel.

Eventually, all of the powder would be sent to Boston to be used at the Battle of Bunker Hill. The HMS Canceaux arrived on December 17th with the HMS Scarborough on the 19th to an emptied fort.

They were too late!

Resource for above information:
The Revolutionary War Journal The First Shots of the American Revolution That Were Not Heard Round the World, October 29, 2018 <u>Historical Background</u>, <u>Organization</u>, <u>Places & Architecture</u>, <u>Weaponry & Munitions</u> Harry Schenawolf